owning a pet
FISH

Selina Wood

SEA-TO-SEA
Mankato Collingwood London

This edition first published in 2008 by
Sea-to-Sea Publications
1980 Lookout Drive
North Mankato
Minnesota 56003

Printed in China

Library of Congress Cataloging
in Publication Data

Wood, Selina.
    Fish / by Selina Wood.
        p.cm. -- (Owning a pet)
    Includes bibliographical references and index.
    ISBN-13 978-1-59771-057-2
    1. Aquarium fishes--Juvenile literature. 2. Aquariums--Juvenile
literature. I. Title. II Series.

SF457.25.W66 2006
639.34--dc22

                             2005056761

9 8 7 6 5 4 3 2

Published by arrangement with the Watts Publishing Group Ltd, London

Series editor: Adrian Cole
Series design: Sarah Borny
Art director: Jonathan Hair
Picture researcher: Kathy Lockley
Special photography: Ray Moller
Illustrations by: Hannah Matthews

The author and publisher would like to thank the following people
for their contribution to the production of this book:

Nat Redfern, Russell, and Ruth, and all the staff at
Chiltern Aquatics, Harlington, England

Acknowledgments:

BE&W/Alamy 11t
Ray Moller 1, 18 t, 19 b, 20 b, 21 b, 21 t, 22, 23 t, 23 b, 29 b, 29 t
Oriental Museum, Durham University/Bridgeman Art Library London,
UK 7
Photomax 6 b, 6 t, 10, 11 b, 12 rc, 13 t, 13 b, 28 t, 28 b & Cover
Rex Features 15 b
Kevin Schafer/Peter Arnold Inc./Alamy 4
Still Pictures /Matt Meadows 27
Maximilian Weinzierl/Alamy 12 tl

WARNING!
The use of chemicals and other water treatments mentioned in this book should be closely supervised by an adult. Always follow the manufacturer's application and safety instructions.

Contents

Pet fish

Fish are fascinating and relaxing to watch. They are relatively inexpensive to keep once their tank or pond environment is established, and most will live for many years.

Fish are sensitive animals that react strongly to small changes in their environment, such as temperature, light levels, and water conditions. Their owner is responsible for all of these things. Before you decide fish are the pets for you, ask yourself if you have the time and money to provide them with the care they deserve.

Suitable fish

Not all fish make suitable pets. You wouldn't be able to keep a leaping salmon in an aquarium! But many species have been specially bred to be pets.

Wild fish, such as these salmon, would not make good pets. Fish species are carefully selected for their suitability as pets.

"I chose fish because I wanted a colorful pet, and I wanted to build a habitat for animals."

Why keep fish?

Looking after fish can be very rewarding. Aquariums are a glimpse of the natural world in the home. You can watch how the fish interact with one another, and how the water and plants sustain them. What's more, you can create and maintain this underwater world yourself.

Make sure keeping fish will fit with how you live and your reasons for wanting a pet in the first place. Many fish are brightly colored, and some have personalities to match. But you can't cuddle them or take them for a walk. Do you have room for an aquarium? If you live in an apartment, are you allowed to have an aquarium? There are many questions like this that need to be answered before owning pet fish.

Large aquariums, such as this one, look stunning but take time to maintain.

From the wild

Breeding conditions can be difficult to create in an aquarium. In the wild some fish give birth to live young, but most fish reproduce by spawning. Only a few of the thousands of eggs survive to grow into adults.

Young fish, called fry, normally emerge from their eggs within days. They stay hidden for several more days in their yolk sacs, before swimming freely to look for food. Some parents protect their eggs and young fry; others leave them to fend for themselves.

The life cycle of fish varies between different species. Many fry grow into adults within weeks; others take a few years to mature fully. Some fish live for just a few months; others more than 30 years. Many wild fish are eaten by predators before they become adults.

Fish eggs on a plant in a tank. Most eggs fail to develop into fish unless kept under the right conditions.

"Fish are cold-blooded, which means that their body temperature becomes the same temperature as their surroundings."

Domestication

Goldfish were probably the first type of fish to be kept in aquariums. Descended from the Crucian Carp, they were bred in China more than 2,000 years ago. You can see goldfish depicted in ancient Asian prints (right) and on fabrics. Today, goldfish are still the most popular of all pet fish.

SHOALING VS SOLITARY

In the wild, most fish live in large groups of their own kind called shoals. If you keep one of these fish alone, it becomes distressed because it feels vulnerable to predators. Other types of fish are solitary and like to hide behind plants and rocks. Some are territorial and bully, or even eat, smaller fish. As a general rule, keep fish of a similar size and temperament together to form a community tank. However, there are exceptions, so research your fish carefully.

Captive breeding

Enthusiasts have kept fish for hundreds of years, but fish-keeping did not take off on a large scale until the twentieth century. Before the widespread use of electricity and the arrival of fast air travel, it was very difficult to transport and look after delicate fish. The first breeding farm for tropical fish opened in Florida in 1926. Since then, the business has grown dramatically, and there are breeding farms across the world, particularly here in the USA and in South East Asia.

Types of fish

There are more than 25,000 species of fish in the world's oceans, lakes, and rivers. Several hundred of these can be bought for home aquariums and ponds.

Not all the same

Not all fish are the same. Most coldwater freshwater fish are suitable for unheated aquariums. Some larger species, such as Koi, can only be kept in ponds. Tropical freshwater fish live in fresh warm water, while marine fish can only survive in saltwater. Many experts suggest that you should not choose marine fish until you have developed your fish-keeping experience.

Tropical freshwater fish

There are about 9,600 kinds of tropical freshwater fish, such as tetras, barbs, and guppies, living in rivers, lakes, and swamps. These are found in Africa, Asia, and South America. Many tropical freshwater fish are imported directly from the countries where they are bred, and a few are still taken directly from the wild. All the species in this category require heated water (see page 17).

Good fish retailers keep a wide range of tropical freshwater fish, such as these clown loaches (see page 13).

Coldwater freshwater fish

Fish from coldwater climates, such as goldfish, barbels, and minnows, can be kept in unheated aquariums. A number of coldwater species can be kept in ponds. All decorative species, such as common goldfish, are bred in controlled conditions. Other species are bred or taken from the wild in regions of Europe, South East Asia, and the USA.

Many coldwater freshwater fish are kept in huge tanks before being sold.

Marine fish

Marine fish live in the salty waters of the world's oceans. Damselfish, angelfish, clownfish, blennies, and gobies can be kept in aquariums as long as they have saltwater. Marine fish are more sensitive to changes in the chemistry of the water than freshwater fish, so they require a lot of care.

AQUARIUM OR POND?

Some fish, such as certain types of goldfish, carp, and Koi, are suitable for garden ponds. Goldfish more than 5 in (12 cm) long are best kept in ponds anyway, because they would be too confined in an aquarium. When you choose pond fish, make sure you select fish that are hardy enough to survive outdoor temperatures, which can reach well below 32°F (0°C) in winter. You should always seek advice at your local fish retailer.

9

Which species?

Choose fish that have a similar temperament to form a community tank. Make good use of the space by selecting fish that swim in the upper level of the tank and some that live lower down.

Coldwater freshwater

Goldfish (left)

Contrary to popular opinion, goldfish need just as much care as any other fish and are not any easier to keep. Some can grow to 8 in (20 cm) long and live longer than ten years. Selective breeding has produced many varieties of these fish, from the hardy common goldfish to more delicate breeds, such as the Fantail, Lionhead, Oranda, Moor, and Shubunkin.

GOLDFISH

Size	**Variable**
Temperament	**Peaceful, shoaling**
Position in tank	**All**
Diet	**Omnivorous**

Cloud minnows

These are small, energetic fish that live in shoals. They are available in different colors and some have gold-tipped fins. They should only be kept with goldfish when they are big enough to avoid being eaten.

CLOUD MINNOWS

Size	**1¼ in (3 cm)**
Temperament	**Peaceful, shoaling**
Position in tank	**Upper**
Diet	**Omnivorous**

Weather loaches (right)

These fish have a green-gray coloring and often have stripes and "freckles." Many people believe they are sensitive to changes in air pressure, which gave them the name "weather" loach.

Tropical freshwater

Platies

These fish are quite short and round, and available in bright colors including orange, yellow, and red. They are easy to look after and breed quickly. They live peacefully with guppies.

WEATHER LOACH

Size	3 in (8 cm)
Temperament	Peaceful
Position in tank	Lower
Diet	Omnivorous

PLATIES

Size	1½ in (4 cm)
Temperament	Peaceful
Position in tank	All
Diet	Omnivorous

Guppies (below left)

Guppies are small fish that are quite easy to keep. They exist in a wide range of colors, males being the more colorful. Guppies prefer hard water and are prone to having their tails nipped by other fish.

GUPPIES

Size	1¼ in (3 cm)
Temperament	Peaceful
Position in tank	All
Diet	Omnivorous

Totally tropical

MOLLIES

Size .... **4 in (10 cm)**
Temperament ..... **Peaceful**
Position in tank .... **All**
Diet .... **Omnivorous**

Mollies (above)

These tropical freshwater fish are quite long and well built. They are available in blends of white, black, and orange. Some males have large "sailfin" dorsal fins.

Tetras (right)

Tetras are small shoaling fish that have shiny, iridescent bodies. They glow in the water as they dart around the tank. To enhance their bright colors, keep them in a dark aquarium.

TETRAS

Size .... **1½–3 in (4–7.5 cm)**
Temperament .... **Peaceful, shoaling**
Position in tank .... **All**
Diet .... **Omnivorous**

Rainbowfish

These beautiful fish are found in a wide variety of colors and sizes. Some have yellow fins, and one type even has bright blue eyes.

RAINBOWFISH

Size .... **3–5 in (7.5–12 cm)**
Temperament ... **Peaceful, shoaling**
Position in tank .... **Middle**
Diet .... **Carnivorous or omnivorous**

Cichlids (above left)

Cichlids exist in various forms; many have very striking markings. They are territorial and can be aggressive, particularly when they are spawning or guarding their young. Some are

CICHLIDS

Size	**5+ in (13+ cm)**
Temperament	**Territorial**
Position in tank	**Middle or lower**
Diet	**Carnivorous or omnivorous**

more gentle than others, so you should seek advice about the species you want.

Barbs

These fish are very active and like to live in a small group, in an aquarium with lots of plants. Common varieties include the Tiger barb and Cherry barb.

BARBS

Size	**1½–4 in (4–10 cm)**
Temperament	**Peaceful, shoaling**
Position in tank	**Middle or lower**
Diet	**Carnivorous or omnivorous**

Clown loaches (right)

These colorful fish are nocturnal and shy. They prefer to lurk in vegetation and can grow to up to 12 in (30 cm).

CLOWN LOACHES

Size	**12 in (30 cm)**
Temperament	**Peaceful, shoaling**
Position in tank	**Lower**
Diet	**Carnivorous**

Finding your fish

You will need to know what fish you want and where to get them, before you buy an aquarium (see pages 16–17). Your tank must be working properly, before you bring your fish home.

Specialist aquarium retailers stock a range of aquarium equipment, as well as fish, and are the best places to buy everything you need. Look for a store that houses its fish in clean tanks, and has knowledgeable staff. Make sure you buy healthy fish. A sick fish could infect your entire tank.

There are many specialist aquarium outlets around the country.

HEALTHY SIGNS

A healthy fish will have:

- **A plump, but not bloated body**

- **A good color (not faded or too dark)**

- **Clear, alert eyes**

- **Intact fins (not torn)**

- **Erect fins (not droopy)**

- **Intact (not swollen) gills**

- **A normal swimming action—not keeling over to one side**

"Don't expect to buy a particular fish from a shoal. Trying to net it will cause the fish too much distress."

Staff at good aquarium retailers will be able to help you choose the right fish.

Ask for more advice

You should already have a good idea about the type of fish you want to buy. But never be afraid to ask for more advice from staff at your aquarium store. Hereare some key questions to ask. How big will my fish be when it is fully grown? What does it like to eat? What type of water does it prefer? Which other fish can it share a tank with?

Traveling home

If you are buying a number of fish at one time, ask if you can buy a special fish box to take them home in. These boxes are usually made from polystyrene, which helps to stop the bag water from cooling too quickly. If you have one or two bags of fish, make sure they are tied securely and that the fish cannot become trapped in the corners of the bag.

FAIRGROUND FISH

Never accept fish from a fairground or amusement park. Often the fish at such places have been kept in poor conditions, and are vulnerable to disease. These fish may die soon after you take them home.

Your aquarium

You need several components to create a healthy coldwater or tropical freshwater aquarium. Once you know what fish you want, find the right equipment to make a perfect environment for them.

Aquariums

Before you buy an aquarium or tank, consider how much room you have at home, how much money you have, and how big your fish will be when fully grown. There are many different types of tank available. Tanks should be wider or longer than they are tall, so that enough oxygen can reach the water surface from the air.

HOW MANY FISH?

Allow an inch (2.5 cm) of tropical fish body for every 12 sq in (75 sq cm) of water surface area. A 24x12 in (60x30 cm) tank holds 24 in (60 cm) of tropical fish in total, and even fewer coldwater fish. You will

You also need to buy lights that will fit your tank—if they are not already built in. Lighting helps your aquarium plants (see page 19) grow, and lets you see the fish inside. You can choose different types of lightbulbs to show your fish at their best.

TANK BASE

Many aquariums come with their own cabinets (left). Or, you can buy special aquarium stands. Whatever you use, it must be strong enough to support the weight of a full tank.

Heater and thermometer

Most tropical freshwater fish live in water at between 72–77° F (22-25° C), so you will need to buy an aquarium heater. Heaters have built-in thermostats that maintain the water temperature so it doesn't become too hot or cold. But be careful when replacing water in the tank. You don't want it to be the wrong temperature because this could harm your fish. You will need a thermometer so you can check your tank is at the correct temperature.

There is a wide range of equipment available to help you set up the perfect aquatic environment.

AIR PUMP

You may also decide to get an air pump. These draw extra oxygen into the water, and push air through an airbrick to aerate the water and improve the water quality.

Filter

Whether you have a coldwater or tropical aquarium, you must have a filter to remove fish waste. Without it your fish will be poisoned by high chemical levels in the water. There are several types of filter available, including an undergravel system driven by a power head, and internal and external power filters. Find out which is best for your tank, fish, and budget.

Setting up

Now that you have your tank equipment, you can begin to put your fish environment together. There is quite a lot to remember, so do it step by step.

Where to put the aquarium

Decide where to put your aquarium before you start because it will be very difficult to move when it is full. Your aquarium should be out of direct sunlight, and somewhere that is not too hot or cold. Also, consider how heavy your tank will be when it is full of water. Don't put it on an unstable floor, and don't put it so high that you can't get at it for regular maintenance. Try to put it near an electrical outlet that can have a circuit breaker installed.

GRAVEL AND ACCESSORIES

- Only use special aquarium gravel for the bottom of your tank.

- Gravel provides a base for aquarium plants and makes the tank look good.

- All aquarium gravel needs to be washed thoroughly before it is placed carefully in the tank.

- All decorations should be soaked in water to remove any dirt.

- Aquarium decorations, such as nontoxic rocks or bogwood, provide shelter for the fish.

Special bogwood adds a natural feature to the aquarium.

There is a huge range of aquarium decorations.

ADDING THE PLANTS

Aquarium plants (right) add beauty and interest to any aquarium. They also help to maintain the balance of chemicals in the water, and offer additional food and shelter for the fish. Safe plants are widely available from your local aquarium retailer. Once you have filled the tank one-quarter full with water, place the roots of the plants in the gravel.

FILL UP THE TANK

Experts advise using "water-balancing" treatment if you use water from the faucet to fill your tank. This reduces the effects that chemicals in the water could have on your fish. Once the tank is full of water, switch on the filter (and the heater of a tropical tank). After 5–10 days, when the filter has matured, the tank will be ready for your fish.

INTRODUCING THE FISH

When you bring fish home they will be distressed. Don't add them straight from the bag into the tank. Give them time to adjust to the tank temperature. Switch the tank lights off and float the bag inside the tank for an hour, being careful to make sure the fish don't get trapped. The water in the bag will reach the same temperature as that in the tank. Hold the bag open and let the fish swim out, being careful to let as little of the bag water out as possible.

Daily routine

Once you have set up your aquarium, get into the routine of feeding your fish every day. Use this time to check that the aquarium is running smoothly.

Fish food

Fish food comes in dried, live, or frozen form. Most high-quality dry fish foods contain a good nutritional balance. These come in flakes, which float on the top of the water for surface feeders, or pellets, which sink for bottom feeders. Some fish need additional nutrients found only in live

(From left to right) Pellet, flake, and freeze-dried fish food are just some of the foods available for fish.

food, such as water fleas or bloodworms. Frozen and freeze-dried fish food is also available. Different species require different diets, so always check what your fish need.

FEEDING TIME

Feed your fish a small amount, twice a day. If there is some uneaten food left after five minutes, it means you are feeding your fish too much. Remove the uneaten food, otherwise it will pollute the water. Make sure surface- and bottom-feeding fish get access to some food.

"My fish know when feeding time is. They rush to the surface before I've even put food in!"

All present and correct

Feeding time is a good opportunity to check that all the fish are present and healthy. Most of the fish should be visible at feeding time, even if they like to feed at different places in the tank. Check for any signs of any sickness or bullying, such as damaged scales or fins. If a fish is missing, look to see if you can find it. It may be unwell and lying somewhere in the tank (see page 29).

Go through the instructions with your fish carer, just to make sure that everything is absolutely clear.

Going on vacation

If you're going away for a few days you can get special blocks of fish food that dissolve gradually over a week. If you go on vacation for longer than a week, then you should ask a friend or neighbor to look after your aquarium.

CARER'S INSTRUCTIONS

Please check my fish every day. Give them two pinches of food and check that they are all feeding well. The pump should be fine, but please check the temperature on the thermometer is still where I've marked it. I've left my uncle's telephone number in case there is a problem.

Aquarium care

Every few days, check that your aquarium equipment is running smoothly, make sure the tank is the correct temperature, and test the water for harmful chemicals.

Algae and plant control

Routinely prune the plants so they don't take over the tank. Be sure to remove any dead leaves before they start to contaminate the water. Keep an eye on algae growth, too. Most algae can be removed with an algae scraper or special chemicals.

Change and check the water

Using a siphon hose and bucket, change 20 percent of the tank water every two weeks. This prevents the buildup of harmful chemicals from the fishes' waste. Balance any faucet water before adding it. Regularly test the pH level, and for chemicals such as ammonia and nitrate.

WATER TESTING KIT

You can buy a water tester to work out the pH (acidity) value of your tank water. Fish prefer a pH value of 7.0–8.0, although most fish are very adaptable. Balance the pH level slowly using special treatment; sudden changes are more likely to kill your fish than high or low acidity.

Use a magnetic scraper to remove algae from the sides of the aquarium to maintain the appearance of your tank.

Clean the filters

Always follow the manufacturer's instructions when you clean your filter. You can clean under the gravel when you change the water by using a gravel vacuum. It siphons out water and waste at the same time. Remember to use water from the tank, not from the faucet, when cleaning parts from the aquarium.

Using a gravel vacuum makes cleaning waste from your aquarium easy. Watch out for any fish that bury themselves, though.

Clean, happy fish!

High or low chemical levels in the water will cause your fish distress. Ask yourself: Is there enough oxygen in the water? (Do you need an air pump?) Is the filter working properly? Are there are too many fish in the tank? Are they overfed? Look after your tank properly and you will have healthy fish.

SIGNS YOUR FISH MAY BE DISTRESSED

- **Gasping for air at the surface**
- **Rubbing against objects**
- **Discoloration of the gills**
- **Swimming very slowly**

Clean water is the key to a healthy tank. It will help reduce the chance of illness and disease.

Your pond

Some types of coldwater freshwater fish, such as goldfish and Koi, can live happily in ponds. Ponds make attractive garden features and are fun to look after.

Which type of pond?

Ponds suitable for fish need to hold water 18–24 in (45-60 cm) deep with a shallower area of 6 in (15 cm) where fish can spawn. There should also be room for plants to grow around the edge. Always seek advice about how many fish your size of pond can hold. They should not be in full sun, or directly under trees.

POND SAFETY

Ponds can be dangerous places, particularly for young children, who can drown in an inch or two of water. To prevent accidents, cover your pond with wire mesh or build a fence around it. These measures will also keep out predators, such as cats and herons.

Buying a liner or precast pond

If you buy a liner you can get exactly the pond shape and size you want, although it is very expensive. Precast plastic ponds are less expensive, but their size cannot be changed. There are many different sizes available (left).

"Whenever I look into the pond, there is always something new to see."

Pump and filter

If you have the money you can fit your pond with a pump and filter. This will improve the water quality and clarity. Even without a filter you can improve the water quality with water plants.

Water plants

Plants help keep the oxygen levels in ponds stable. At the bottom of the pond, plant some "oxygenators," such as hornwort. These plants give out lots of oxygen in daylight. Floating plants, such as water soldier, provide shade and shelter for the fish and make an attractive addition to the pond. Around the edge, place some "emergent" plants, such as arrowhead, to provide a spawning place for the fish.

There are many types of water plant. Oxygenating plants improve the water quality for fish.

Water snails

It is normal for your pond to have some algae growing in it, but if it gets out of control, you may need to remove some of it yourself. Or, you can introduce some water snails. They feed on algae, but they also like to eat water plants, so you will have to keep an eye on them!

Pond care

Although ponds rely on the natural elements to sustain them, they still require regular maintenance if your fish are to thrive. Here are some routine care tips:

Feeding pond fish

How much you feed your pond fish varies according to the water temperature. Generally, you should feed them once a day in summer, three to four times a week in spring and during the fall, and not at all in winter. Pond fish don't feed during the winter because they hibernate at the bottom of the pond.

Essential pond cleaning

It is important to remove all dead leaves and excess algae, because these upset the chemistry of the water. Prune the pond plants regularly so they don't take over too much of the pond and block out the sun. Every so often, test the water for harmful chemicals. About once a year, clear out the pond completely and check to see if any repairs are needed.

This formal pond has both oxygenating plants and lilies. You can see the fish swimming beneath the surface.

Water refill

Long spells of hot weather in summer may cause some of the water from your pond to evaporate. You will need to fill it back up. Always make sure you leave faucet water to stand for 24 hours to dechlorinate before adding it to the pond. Or, you can use rainwater from a water butt.

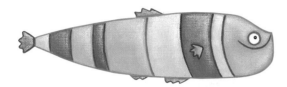

Pond life

Ponds are great places for watching wildlife. Many animals gravitate to ponds. Birds may drink or bathe in the water, frogs and toads may spawn there, and dragonflies and water boatmen may skim over the water. A well functioning pond teems with life.

Coping with ice

You can prevent a pond from icing over in winter by using a pond cover, or an anti-ice device. A cheaper way is to float a ball in the pond, so that if the water freezes, you can take the ball out, leaving a gap for the fish to breathe through. Never smash ice on a pond. The shock waves that are sent through the water could kill your fish.

POND DO'S AND DON'TS

DO position your pond in a sheltered place, but not under a large tree.

DO plant oxygenating plants.

DO clear leaves from the surface of the water.

DON'T use chemicals in the garden; they could wash into the water and poison it.

DON'T overfeed your pond fish.

Frogs soon find their way to ponds. Make sure they can get in and out of your pond by building a small ramp.

Healthy fish

Even if you keep your aquarium or pond in excellent condition, it is likely that at some stage one of your fish will get sick. Watch out for signs of illness and deal with them immediately.

SIGNS YOUR FISH MAY BE UNWELL:

- white tufts on the body and mouth may be due to a fungal or bacterial infection—this can be fatal

- trailing feces in the water may be a sign that the fish is constipated—its diet is not well balanced

- white spots over the skin, fins, and gills can indicate a serious but often treatable disease

- tears in the fins caused by fin rot

- very bloated body (above, left)

- protruding eyes

- loss of color

- skin tumors

- loss of balance

- droopy fins (below)

If your fish gets any of these symptoms you should seek advice from a fish expert. Fish diseases are often treatable if they are caught early. Less serious infections can be easily dealt with using treatments from an aquarium store.

TOP TIPS

Remember that fish are more likely to become diseased if their environment is not looked after properly or the wrong types of fish are living together. You should:

- Buy from an aquarium retailer.

- Clean the tank regularly. This varies depending on the number of fish and the size of your tank. If there are feces or algae in your tank it already needs cleaning!

- Check that the filters and heater (if used) are working properly.

- Regularly check the pH and chemistry of the water using a water kit (see page 22).

- Avoid overcrowding (see page 16).

- Avoid overfeeding (see page 20).

- Don't put territorial fish with peaceful fish (see page 7).

Quarantine tank

It is a good idea to have a small tank in addition to your main aquarium. This can be used to put diseased fish in while they recover and to quarantine new fish that you buy, in case they have a disease.

Illness and death

There will come a time when one of your fish becomes too sick to treat or dies of old age. Many fish keepers think that the kindest thing to do is to kill it humanely. If you can't do it, ask an adult (see below).

PAINLESS DEATH

Never flush a fish down a toilet or leave it to suffocate out of water. These methods are cruel. Many experts believe the most painless way to kill a terminally ill fish is to put it in a water-filled, disposable, plastic container (such as an old margarine carton) and place it in a freezer. Over a few hours, the fish will slowly fall asleep and die.

Glossary

Aerate: To pass air through water, for example, using an air pump and airbrick. It increases the water oxygen level.

Chemicals: Substances in pond or aquarium water that affect the water quality.

Community tank: An aquarium that has a good mixture of fish with similiar, peaceful temperaments.

Dorsal fin: The large, upright fin found on the top of fishes' bodies.

Emergent: A plant that grows around the edge of a pond.

Evaporate: To change water into a gas through heating.

Freshwater: Coming from rivers, lakes, and swamps; not saltwater.

Fry: Young fish, especially when newly hatched.

Gills: Breathing organs of fish that take oxygen out of water allowing them to breathe.

Hibernate: To fall into a deep sleep during the cold winter months.

Marine: Coming from the sea.

Nutrients: The different components of food that give an animal energy and help keep it well.

Oxygenator: A water plant that enriches the water with oxygen.

pH: A scale used to measure the amount of acid or alkalinity in a liquid ranging from 0 (very acidic) to 14 (very alkaline). Water generally has a pH level of 7.

Quarantine: To keep an animal separate from others to prevent the spread of disease.

Shoal: A large group of fish.

Spawn: To produce and deposit eggs. Also means a large number of fry produced by a fish.

Species: A group of animals that have common characteristics that are distinct from other animals, and that can reproduce with one another.

Tropical: From the hot, humid climate of the tropics.

Websites

If you would like further advice on how to keep fish, or information on aquarium clubs, contact staff at your local aquarium retailer. Information is also available on the Internet. Some useful websites are listed below:

Aquaria Organizations and Societies:
www.fishprofiles.net/faq/organizations.asp
This website lists national and international aquarium societies, as well as local societies.

www.fishkeeping.co.uk
This website provides information for keeping coldwater and tropical freshwater fish, including care guides, news articles, and an image gallery.

www.aquariumhobbyist.com
This website contains a wealth of information from product reviews to care sheets and frequently asked questions. Also features a section on pet loss.

www.practicalfishkeeping.co.uk
Website of *Practical Fishkeeping* magazine, featuring up-to-date news articles on all types of aquarium and pond-based fish.

www.tfhmagazine.com
The website of the popular American magazine *Tropical Fish Hobbyist*, has accurate, fascinating, up-to-the-minute information on the aquarium hobby, from small freshwater tanks to wall-sized reef tanks and landscaped ponds. It is aimed at the expert as well as the beginner.

More general information on the care, health, and welfare of pets is available from a number of organizations. These include:

RSPCA (Royal Society for the Prevention of Cruelty to Animals)
www.rspca.co.uk
The RSPCA runs animal hospitals and shelters for sick and homeless animals across the world. It rehomes animals, runs a public advice line, investigates suspected cases of cruelty, and inspects conditions animals are kept in.

www.aspca.org
The American Society for the Prevention of Cruelty to Animals' website provides a comprehensive guide for the first-time fishkeeper, listing everything you will need to know, and including a fish supply checklist.

Every effort has been made by the Publishers to ensure that these websites contain no inappropriate or offensive material. However, because of the nature of the Internet, it is impossible to guarantee the contents of these sites will not be altered. We strongly advise that Internet access is supervised by a responsible adult.

Index